INVENTOR. WILLARD B. PAINE CLUTCH OPERATING MECHANISM Patent N. 2,168,682 Filed Sept. 23, 1933

Willard the Executive Engineer

Written by Lori Lorenz

with Carolyn Paine Bower and Willard Baker Paine, Jr.

Illustrated by Savannah Philyaw

Willard was born April 26, 1905. He grew up in the small town of Winthrop, a bulbous peninsula just outside Boston, Massachusetts. Willard's father was a salesman, and his mom made a comfortable home for their small family. Willard was a curious boy who liked to figure out how things worked, and was especially interested in anything having to do with the newly invented automobile.

Willard was a good student and wanted to be the first person in his family to go to college. During a trip to Boston, Willard looked across the Charles River at the Massachusetts Institute of Technology (MIT). Willard dreamed of attending MIT to become an engineer. His parents saved their money to send him to a special preparatory school, and Willard studied extra hard to be accepted to this prestigious college.

Willard would be prepared when this opportunity came his way.

Willard graduated from MIT during the Great Depression. Even with a college degree, it was very difficult to find a job.
Willard was determined and was able to find a position with the Bendix Corporation. He was excited to join a company that built parts for automobiles. One of Willard's inventions was a new safety feature for car brakes.

Due to his hard work, Willard was offered a promotion to chief engineer. Willard was pleased that his career was progressing. Maybe one day he would work his way up to an executive position!

Willard would be prepared when this opportunity came his way.

Willard married Marjorie, a beautiful and clever girl, also from Winthrop, who was known as "Midge". She had two sisters, Dora and Beulah. Each of them played a musical instrument, and the three of them often performed at house parties and dances. Midge had a gift for entertaining and looked forward to supporting Willard as he advanced in his career.

Midge was also an excellent seamstress. She knew that being a successful executive's wife meant creating a nice home and making sure they were dressed properly for all occasions. She would have to be creative during the depression when money was tight.

Midge would be prepared when this opportunity came her way.

World War II began for America with the bombing of Pearl Harbor on December 7, 1941. Everyone rallied to help fight the war. The Bendix Corporation shifted from making car parts to airplane parts for our B-17 and B-24 bomber airplanes. Willard was promoted to general manager and asked to take on the responsibility of leading a new manufacturing plant. This was an important promotion for Willard—his first executive position.

Bendix
H. POCKETS
Willard B. Paine
GENERAL MANAGER

The Bendix plant was located near the place where the airplanes were assembled. Army Air Corps pilots would then fly the new bombers over to Europe and Japan to help fight the war.

Willard was proud to serve the war effort when this opportunity came his way.

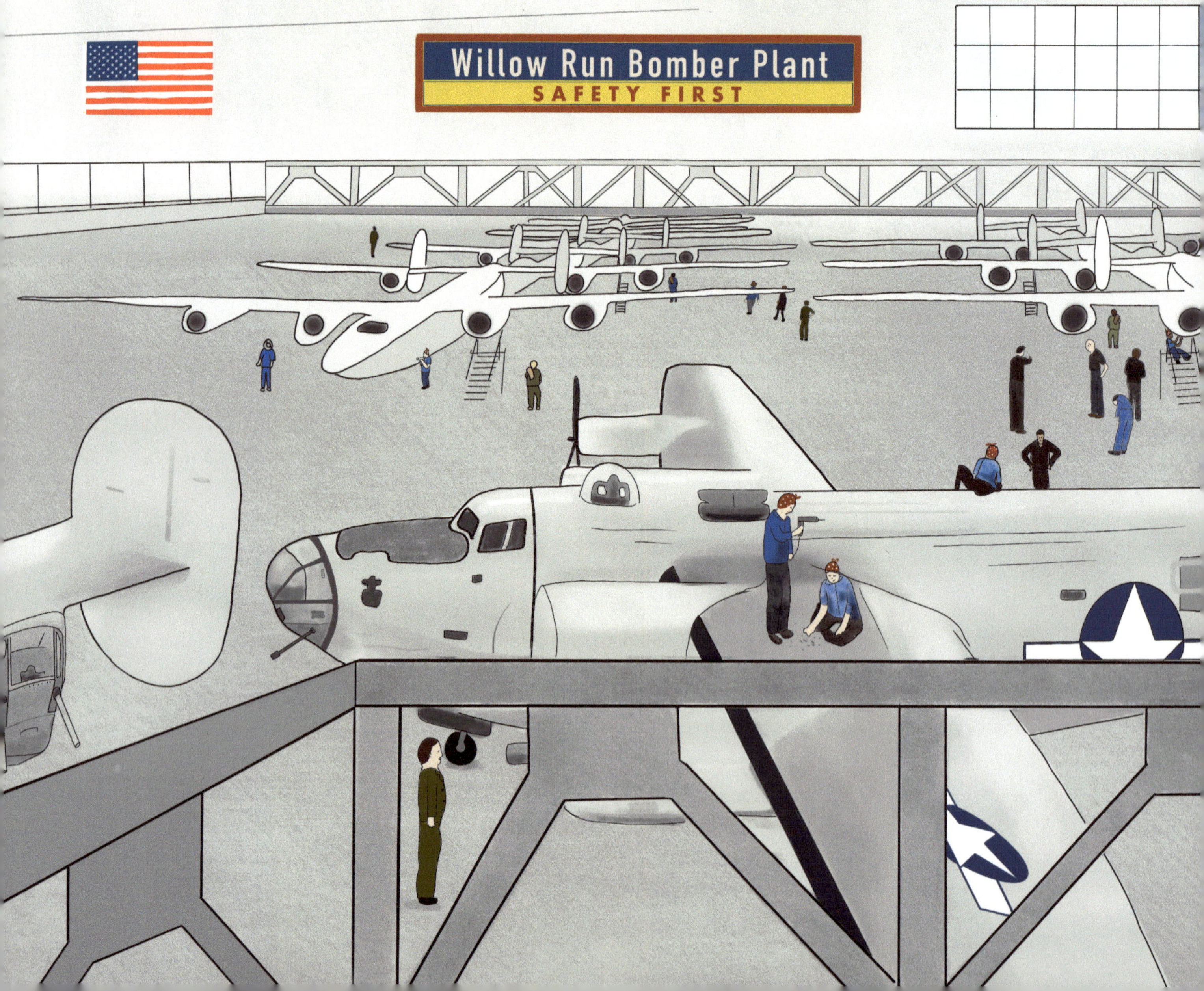

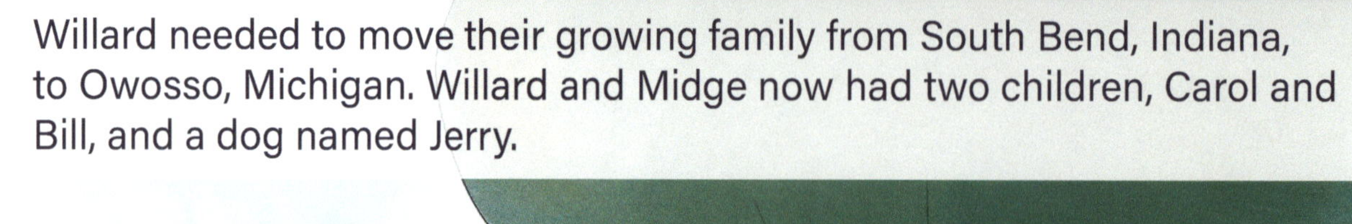

Willard needed to move their growing family from South Bend, Indiana, to Owosso, Michigan. Willard and Midge now had two children, Carol and Bill, and a dog named Jerry.

Bendix found a unique place for Willard and his family to live called The Curwood House. Built by a famous author of adventure stories, James Oliver Curwood, the house was twice the size of most houses with the yard taking up an entire city block! Willard and Midge were ready to make the most of their opportunity to live in this special place.

Peter and the Wolf

Midge got busy making the large and unique house into their home. They didn't have enough furniture for all the rooms, so she solved the problem by using one living room for the summer and one for the winter. This meant that each season the family would move all the furniture from one side of the house to the other.

Midge began hosting neighbors and friends for Saturday night dinners. Food was rationed during the war, so the meals were potluck, where everybody brought something to share. Everyone was doing their part to help America win the war.

Midge was pleased she had a home big enough to take advantage of this opportunity to help make the war years a little happier for their community.

Simplicity PRINTED Pattern 35¢
C U

The Curwood House had a large attic on the third floor. It was Carol's favorite place to play. She spent hours designing new outfits for her paper doll family. Carol also had two baby dolls, Jane and Ruth. She was a good mom to her dolls, especially Ruth who had a broken foot.

Jane and Ruth sat with Carol at dinner every night since her dad worked late and Bill was already in bed. Carol dreamed of having her own family one day that would sit around the dinner table together.

Carol would be prepared when this opportunity came her way.

Carol loved school. She was an excellent student and worked hard to please her teachers and her parents. They were very proud of her. One morning when Carol and her friends were walking to school, they saw smoke. The school was on fire! The firefighters were able to put it out, but the school was damaged and they had to be in a temporary classroom until a new school could be built.

Even as a toddler, Bill loved everything about cars, trucks, or anything on wheels. He rode his truck around the house and couldn't wait to be old enough to drive a real car.

One day Bill decided to "drive" his truck to the Curwood Castle on the other side of the river. He was not supposed to leave the yard, but Bill wasn't very good at following the rules, especially when his curiosity got the best of him. Can you guess what happened?

Bill rolled down the lawn and across the street. It was winter so the river was covered in ice. He was too young to understand the danger as he tried to drive his truck across the frozen river. Uh oh!

You guessed it, Bill fell through the ice into the cold river! Luckily, Carol was nearby and called for help, and Bill was pulled to safety. He got a scolding for leaving the yard, but Bill got a taste of freedom that day and dreamed of a time when he would have the opportunity to see the world from a real motor vehicle.

Bill would be prepared when this opportunity came his way.

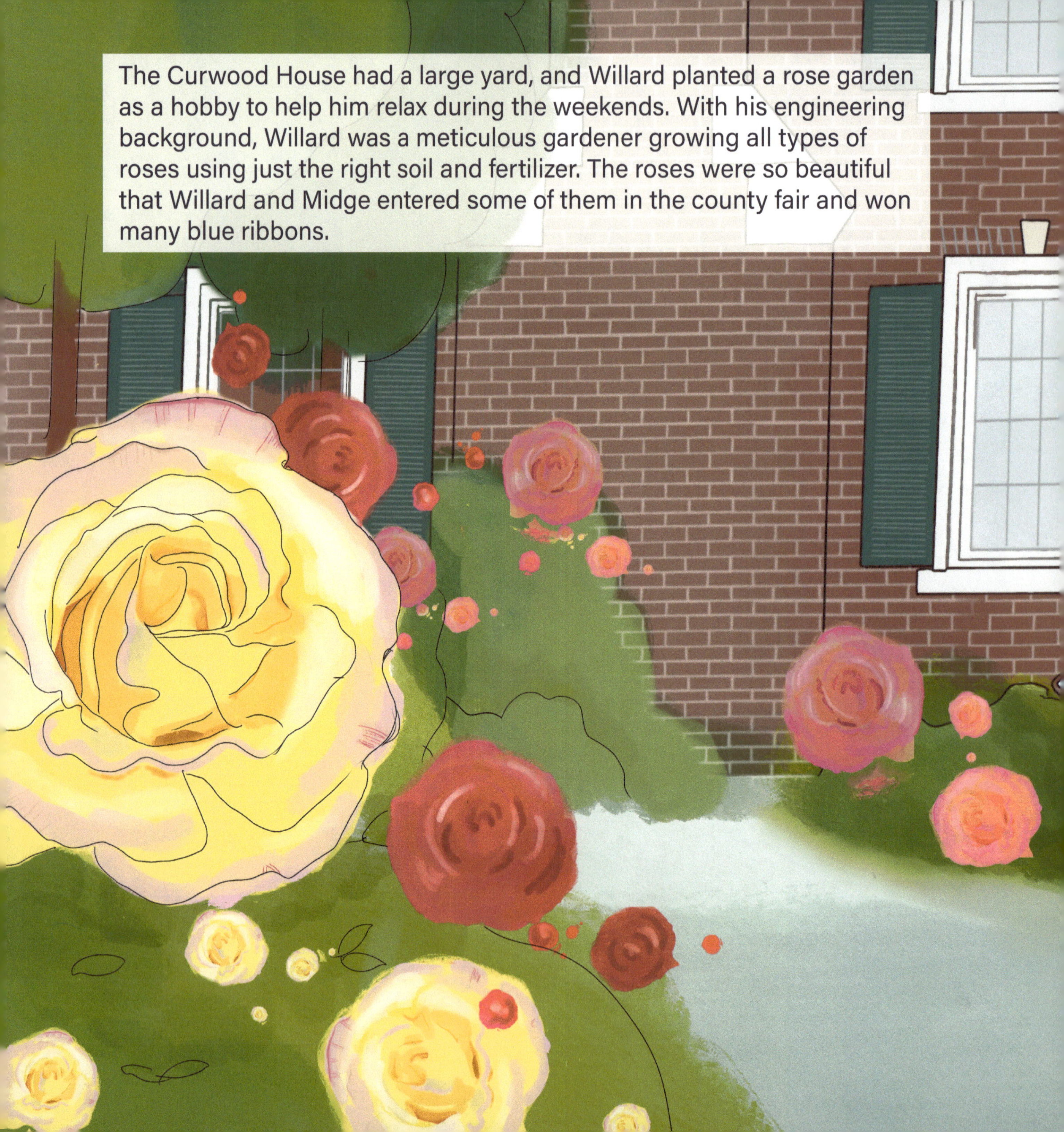

The Curwood House had a large yard, and Willard planted a rose garden as a hobby to help him relax during the weekends. With his engineering background, Willard was a meticulous gardener growing all types of roses using just the right soil and fertilizer. The roses were so beautiful that Willard and Midge entered some of them in the county fair and won many blue ribbons.

Willard went out to the rose garden every morning to clip roses for his staff at the Bendix plant. Midge would help arrange them, happy for the opportunity to add some cheer to the people working such long hours to help America win the war.

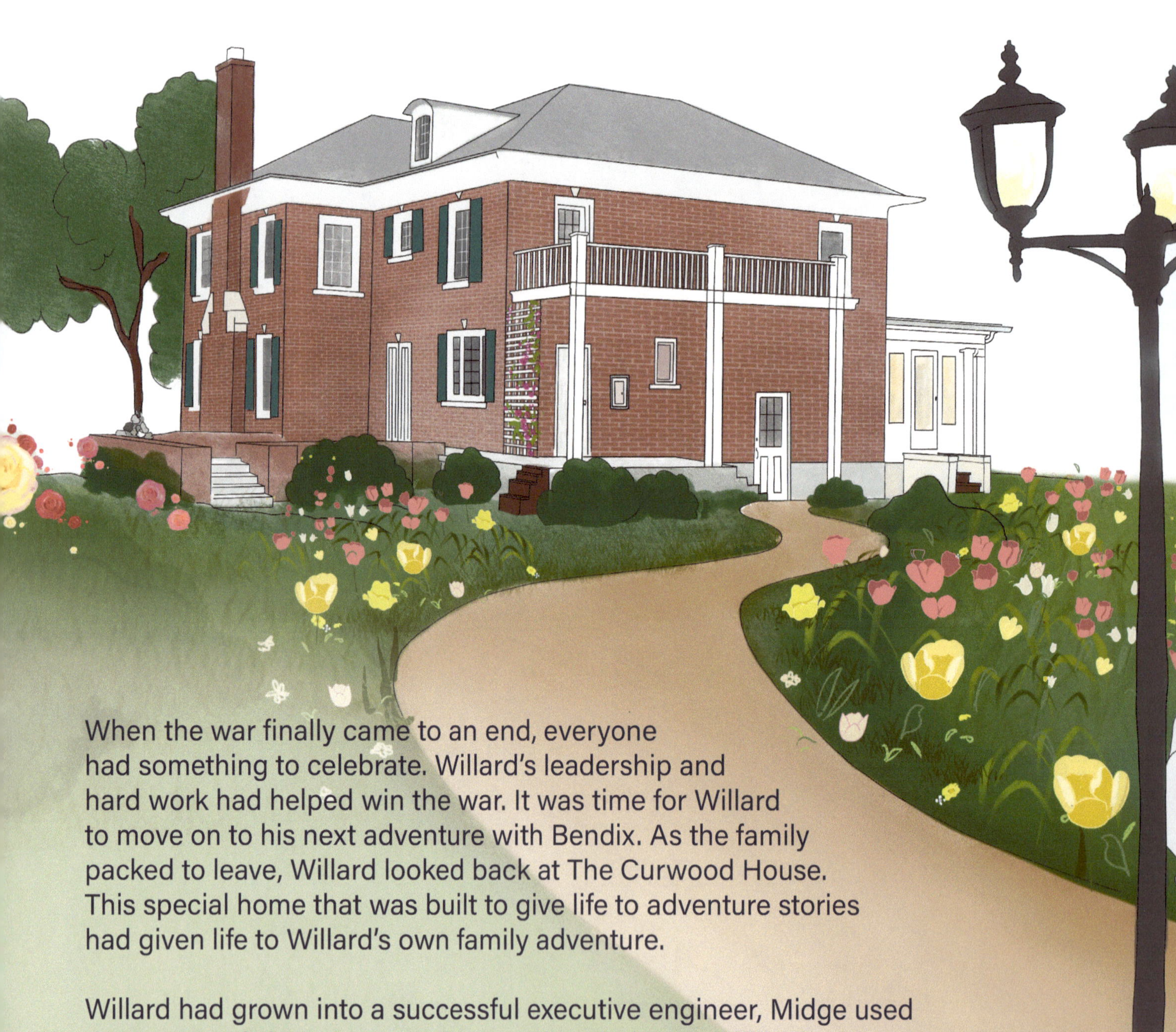

When the war finally came to an end, everyone had something to celebrate. Willard's leadership and hard work had helped win the war. It was time for Willard to move on to his next adventure with Bendix. As the family packed to leave, Willard looked back at The Curwood House. This special home that was built to give life to adventure stories had given life to Willard's own family adventure.

Willard had grown into a successful executive engineer, Midge used the space to bring a community together during the difficult war years, and Carol and Bill found plenty of room to begin chasing their own dreams.

About Willard the Executive Engineer & His Family

Willard Baker Paine was born April 26, 1905, in Malden, Massachusetts, to Lydia May MacDonald and Alfred James Paine. Willard grew up in Winthrop and graduated from Winthrop High School, with an extra year at The Governor's Academy, a boarding school that Willard's parents worked hard to afford in order to prepare Willard for college—a first in his family.

Willard attended MIT and graduated in 1930 with a Bachelor of Science degree in Mechanical Engineering. Willard had multiple job offers and was proud to accept one from his first choice, Bendix Corporation. During his post-graduation vacation in Maine, Willard received a letter from Bendix, rescinding the offer due to the oncoming depression. As a testament to his determination and work ethic, Willard returned to MIT immediately to arrange for another position from one of his backup offers, the American Can Company. It was a terrible disappointment, but Willard had grown up tough. Due to an accident in his childhood, Willard had a disabled leg that left him with a permanent limp, unable to run, participate in sports, or enlist in the military. He was also born left-handed, but had been trained to use his right hand in order to fit in. Willard expected a lot from himself and others, yet greeted the world with a grin and a sense of humor. Within a year, Bendix had reoffered a position, and Willard was off to South Bend, Indiana to begin a long and successful career with the Bendix Corporation and later, Bendix-Westinghouse.

In 1932, Willard married Marjorie Jane Barkley. Midge was beautiful, talented, smart, and would prove to be an excellent partner for Willard's growing career. They had two children while in South Bend, Carolyn Barkley Paine in 1936 and Willard Baker Paine Jr (Bill) in 1940.

Willard was a successful engineer. He was promoted to chief engineer and had multiple patents to his name. When World War II began, he was asked to move to Owosso, Michigan, to run a new wartime division of Bendix which would manufacture aviation equipment for bombers, including gun turrets for the B-17 and B-24 bombers. Willard would make many trips to Henry Ford's nearby Willow Run Bomber Plant, where the bombers were assembled in a unique facility that turned out an airplane every sixty-three minutes. He found that his excellent engineering education did not properly prepare him for the management and leadership positions into which he was being promoted. However, Willard's strong work ethic and sheer determination once again served him well. He hired talented people and spent long hours at the office to ensure success for Bendix and for the war effort.

A unique house was available for Willard and his family in Owosso—the former estate of James Oliver Curwood. One of Owosso's most famous residents, Curwood was an author of wilderness adventure stories and a conservationist. Curwood built his home in 1909 and a small castle nearby, which he used as his office. The home had sat empty since Curwood's death in 1927. The city controlled the house while it was in a long period of probate. Due to the lingering depression, no one could afford to rent the home, much less buy it. The city offered this beautiful home on its acre of land to the Paine family for only $40/month. Just enough to cover the cost of the property taxes.

The house was much larger than the Paine family needed and had more rooms than they could furnish but had plenty of space to house a growing career, an expanding life, and young children's dreams. Many memories have been recounted of the Paine's time in Owosso in that magnificent home. Willard and Midge entertained often, although wartime entertaining was always potluck due to rationing. The Paine parties were a nice reprieve for these industry leaders from the difficult days of World War II.

This special house that had given life to many adventure stories would give life to Willard's executive career, Midge's flair for being a hostess, Carol's dreams of a family of her own, and Bill's sense of adventure and love for all things on wheels.

Carol was an excellent student and spent hours in the large attic playing with her dolls, including sitting with them every night at her little dinner table in the kitchen while her mom waited for her dad to arrive home from work. Carol went to college at University of Colorado, earning her Phi Beta Kappa key for scholarship and eventually her master's degree. She had a successful career of her own as a schoolteacher and State Farm agent. More importantly, her dream of becoming a mom came true five times over, and she and her family shared many happy hours around the family dinner table, just as she had imagined.

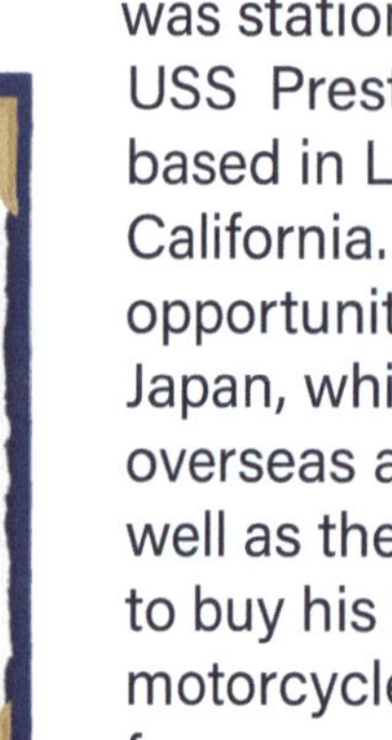

Bill felt his dream came true when he took his first road trip at sixteen in his mom's 1957 Ford Thunderbird. He had prepared for college but decided to join the Navy. After basic training and advanced electronics school, Bill was stationed on the USS Preston, a destroyer based in Long Beach, California. He had the opportunity to serve in Japan, which offered overseas adventure as well as the opportunity to buy his first Honda motorcycle. He left the Navy with a plan for his life. Over the next few years, Bill would complete his degree in marketing from California State University at Long Beach, meet and marry his wife, open Pacific Coast Honda motorcycle shop, and welcome a daughter into their family. Bill went on to run the service department at Bill Krause Honda, then opened his own shop which he ran for twenty years with his daughter at his side. Bill has driven his family over 160,000 miles, seeing America and Canada from behind the wheel of their RV, "Wally."

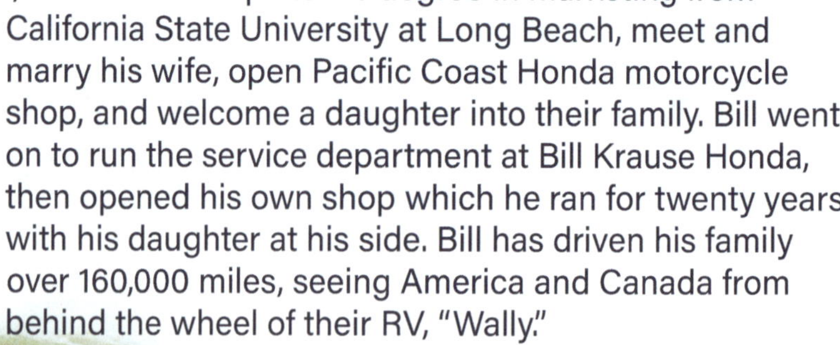

In 1947, Willard's career took him to Kansas City where he was the general manager of a Bendix Aviation plant devoted exclusively to the manufacture of complex equipment for the weapons program of the Atomic Energy Commission. In 1957, the Paine family moved to Elyria, Ohio, until Willard's retirement in 1969 as president and CEO of Bendix-Westinghouse. Truly a successful executive who never left his engineering roots.

In his spare time, Willard enjoyed woodworking and cultivating his vast rose garden. While Willard found these creative hobbies relaxing, his "faultless and accurate" engineering approach resulted in award-winning roses and creation of a unique miniature grandfather clock that serves as an individual heirloom for each of his children and grandchildren.

April 26, 1905 - May 27, 1986

Willard and Midge retired to La Jolla, California, where they spent many enjoyable years with Carol and Bill and their families. In 1982, Willard and Midge celebrated their fiftieth golden wedding anniversary at a lovely party at their Kona Kai Club hosted by Carol and Bill.

Note: Willard Baker Paine is a descendent of John Howland and Elizabeth Tilley, two of the Mayflower passengers who eventually married and now have over ten million descendants. Their story can be found in John and Elizabeth, the Mayflower Pilgrims in the Ancestor Adventure Series.

Dedication

For my mom, Carol, who always knew she wanted to be a mom, and whose faith, love, determination, and grit have set an example for each of us as we chased our own dreams.

Author's Note

Willard the Executive Engineer was inspired by family stories my grandparents shared about their unique time in Owosso, Michigan, during World War II in The Curwood House.

On her eighty-fifth birthday, Carol invited her brother, Bill, and their families back to The Curwood House in Owosso for a magical long weekend birthday event. We saw the attic, slept in the family bedrooms, and gathered around the kitchen table, imagining the way it must have been during a time when so many were working so hard for freedom and opportunity, and celebrated the role this special house played during that era in our family history.

Gratitude

I am grateful for the creative collaboration with my co-authors, my mom, Carol, and my Uncle Bill. Their memories of the parties, the fall in the river, the magical attic playroom, and the Bendix work at Willow Run were key elements of this grand adventure. Our goddaughter Savannah's beautiful illustrations brought this magnificent home and the events during the war years to life. Her work used the smallest of details to truly capture the grandness of this adventure for the Paine family.

Michelle, the current owner of The Curwood House, hosted us twice as we celebrated my mom's birthday and returned with Savannah to begin the illustration work. We would highly recommend a stay at this beautiful bed and breakfast. (TheCurwoodHouse.com). During one trip, we had an unexpected opportunity to tour the Yankee Air Museum at Willow Run. Our guide, Michael, delighted us with an opportunity to imagine the important war work that took place there. (For more information, please visit YankeeAirMuseum.org). Piper, the Director at the Shiawassee Arts Center (SAC) was very helpful with the history of Bendix in Owosso, including uncovering a photo showing the women employees – Owosso's own "Rosie the Riveters". (More information on the SAC's purpose, plus a photo of her adorable dog, Jacks, can be found on their website ShiawasseeArts.org).

And to my husband, Paul, whose enthusiasm for the project and "faultless and accurate" assistance with the engineering and technical details made all the difference in this labor of love.

Truly, it doesn't get any better than this.

Ancestor Adventure Series

The Ancestor Adventure Series celebrates the adventurous spirit of our ancestors whose courage and bravery helped them forge a better life for themselves and future generations. Whatever dreams they chased and hardships they encountered, the stories of our ancestors are full of excitement and life lessons.

May they inspire you to take your own grand adventure.

Books in the Ancestor Adventure Series:

Book 1 - *Larry the Blue Water Sailor*
Join Larry as he prepares to fulfill his lifelong dream of sailing to the South Pacific, finding joy in every moment leading up to his grand adventure.

Book 2 - *Willard the Executive Engineer*
Join Willard and his family as they take up residence in The Curwood House, a unique estate that offers a retreat during World War II, while providing the next generation room to dream.

Book 3 - *Ed the Gold Prospector - Coming Soon*
Join Ed as he heads to the wild west of Victor, Colorado to seek his fortune, managing to strike pure gold along the way.

www.ingramcontent.com/pod-product-compliance
Lightning Source LLC
Chambersburg PA
CBHW042106110726
48006CB00002B/542

* 9 7 9 8 8 3 6 3 0 7 9 0 5 *